omera

engage. encourage. empower.

The Conquest of Banger the Cat

By Annie Mack
Illustrated by Phillip Reed

OMERA PRESS LTD

Annie Mack Publications Division

*"In loving memory of my sweet Banger.
It was an honour to serve you!"*

At first, family and friends would ask, "Who's Banger?"
Our response, "The cat." And that is how Banger, the cat, came to be.
Other aliases:
Mr. Bittersworth
Bitter Bang
King Big Bang
Roi Banger, le chat
Pretty Boy

First published in 2024 by Omera Press Ltd.

This is a work of fiction. Names, characters, places, and incidents are either the product of the author's imagination or are used fictitiously. Any resemblance to actual persons, living or dead, events, or locales is entirely coincidental.

Text copyright © 2024 Annie Mack
Cover art and interior illustrations copyright © 2024 Phillip Reed
Edited by Kara Cybanski

This publication is protected by copyright law. All rights are reserved. No portion of this work may be duplicated, stored within a retrieval system, or disseminated, by any method or medium (including electronic, mechanical, photocopying, recording, or any other means), without the explicit prior written consent of the publisher. Unauthorized actions in relation to this publication may result in both criminal prosecution and civil litigation for potential damages.

Published in Canada by Omera Press – Annie Mack Publications, a children's book division of Omera Press, Guelph, ON.

Visit us on the Web!
www.omerapress.com

ISBN
Electronic: 978-1-7381529-4-0
Paperback: 978-1-7381529-3-3

Do you have a pet?

I didn't exactly plan to have a furry friend when my best friend Mick and I moved out West for our school's work-study program. But that changed when a **stray** cat walked into our ground floor apartment with all the grace and determination that you know only a **cat** could muster.

This is the story of how we became **pet owners**...

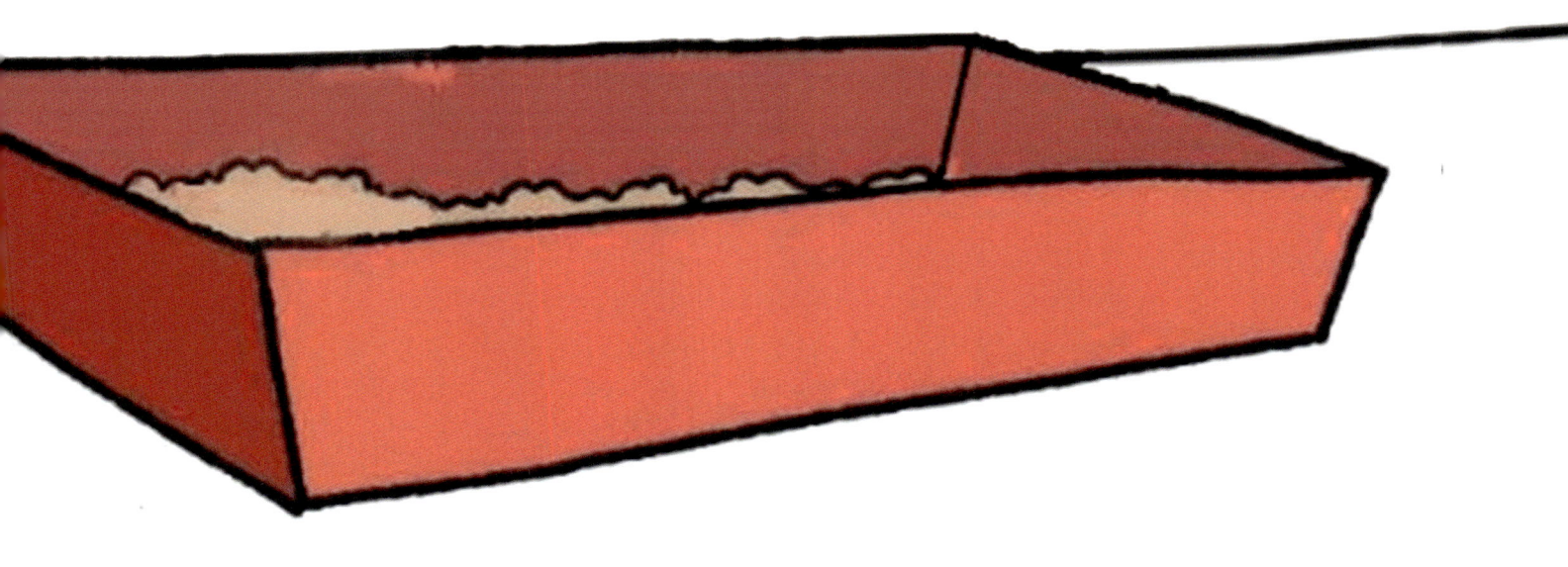

We came from the **East**
to live in the **West**
for our co-op program.
We felt this would be best.

We moved in our boxes
and sat on the floor.
I think it was Mick
who left **open** the door.

We who were *two*,
that day became *three*.
I'll tell you of how
it all came to be.

While unpacking items
to sort this and that,
we both looked up, startled,
when in strolled a cat.

He looked up and down,
must have **liked** what he saw.
'Cause he flopped to the ground,
and then held out his **paw**.

I looked in his eyes.
I knew that was that.
We had just been **adopted**
by this poor shabby cat.

Headfirst he'd dash
with a daring flare.
No time for pauses,
he'd ZOOM everywhere.
With a bump and a thump,
he'd charge ahead,
like a mischief maker
with plans to spread.

He would skid across
the kitchen floor,
Then **CRASH**! He'd hit
the cupboard door.
He would bang into this
and bang into that.
We knew right then,
he was **Banger** the cat.

Banger wasted no time making himself at **home**.

The rooms were **inspected**, all over he'd roam,

'til he marked every corner
of our little flat.
To him, it **belonged**
to Banger the cat.

He came all infested with **fleas** and things
that **bit** at our ankles and crawled under his skin.
Our apartment was plagued with this and with that.
So, off to the vet **sulked** Banger the cat.

We built him a **perch**, made of carpet and wood.

He immediately took over.

It was well understood

that this throne was now **his**.

There was no welcome mat.

He **safeguarded** his kingdom

as *Roi Banger, le chat!*

Banger had **charm**.
More than most cats, I'd say.
He'd **tempt** you with love,
and then take it away.

But when paid no attention
he gave us a pat!
How dare we *ignore* him
Poor Banger the cat.

Bitter Bang and **Mr. Bitters**
were some of the names
he was called when he **snubbed**
all the high-priced cat games.

Just a **yarn ball** or shoebox
amused this spoiled brat.
So **simple** a creature
was Banger the cat.

When I laid on my stomach, all cozy in bed,

he'd crawl on my back and swat at my head.

"*Get up! Feed me now!*" he meowed in a spat.

I'd give in just to stop more torment from this cat.

He'd **follow** me around, wherever I'd go. "*Where is my* **feeder**?" he wanted to know.

But believe me, in his mind
'twas more than just that.
"I *make the* **rules**!"
thought Banger the cat.

"IT'S FEED ME TIME"

If he felt my **assignments**
were taking too long,
Banger sat on my books.
It was time to **move** on.

He would swat the mouse
right off of my desk.
"*You can play on the Net
when I go for a **rest**.*"

One day we **returned** from shopping in town.
We searched the flat,
but Banger wasn't around.
Then I looked in the loo and to my **surprise**,
I discovered the toilet roll
shrunken in size.

While I cleaned out his **litter**, he'd wait by the door
until I was finished. Then, he'd **unload** some more.
He'd strut on past me, proving just that:
I was the **servant** of Banger the cat.

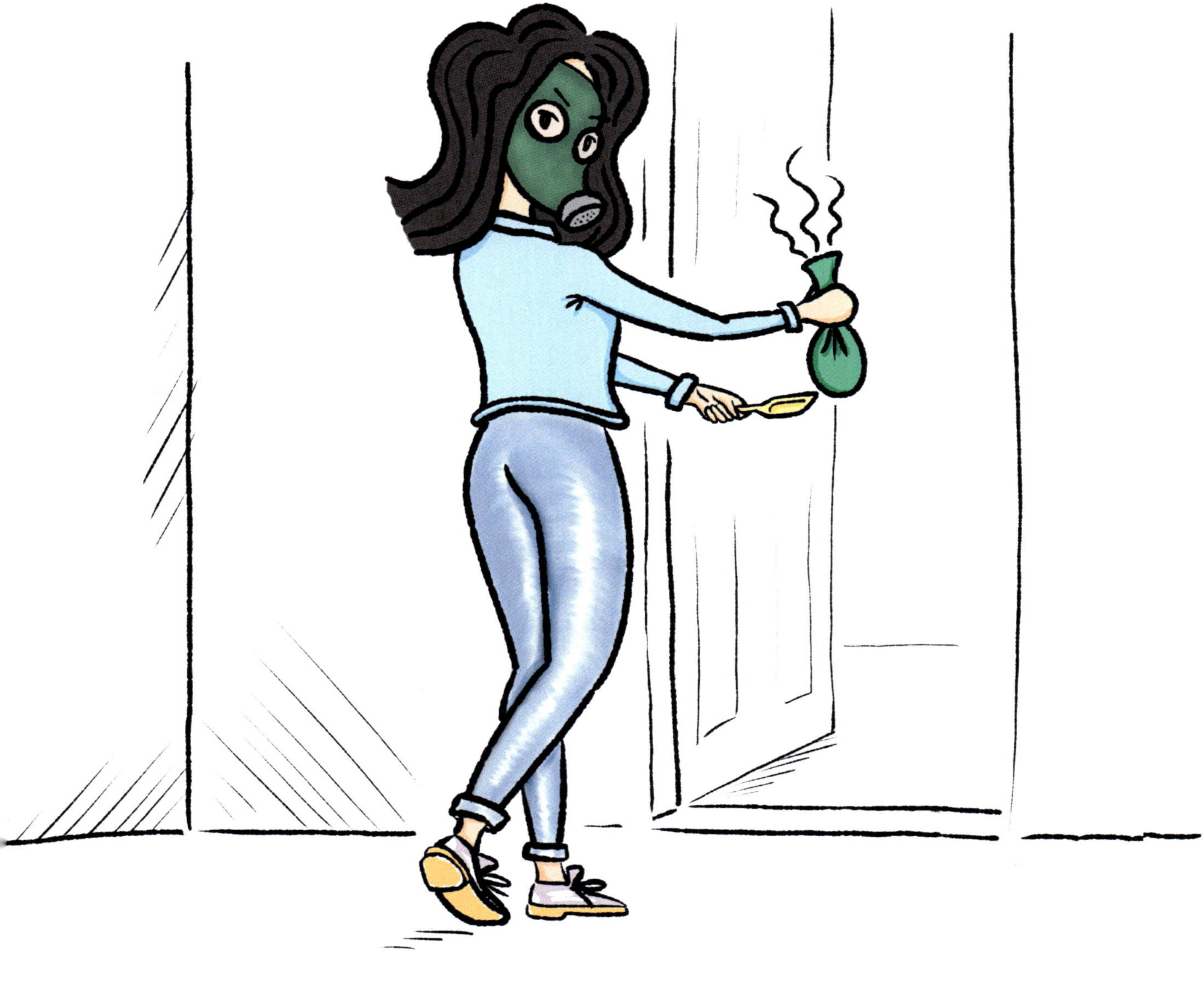

Mick took my place when I was away.

But when I returned, Mick got **no time** of day.

Banger had **skills** like a smart diplomat.

Playing on his cuteness, he was a **master** at that.

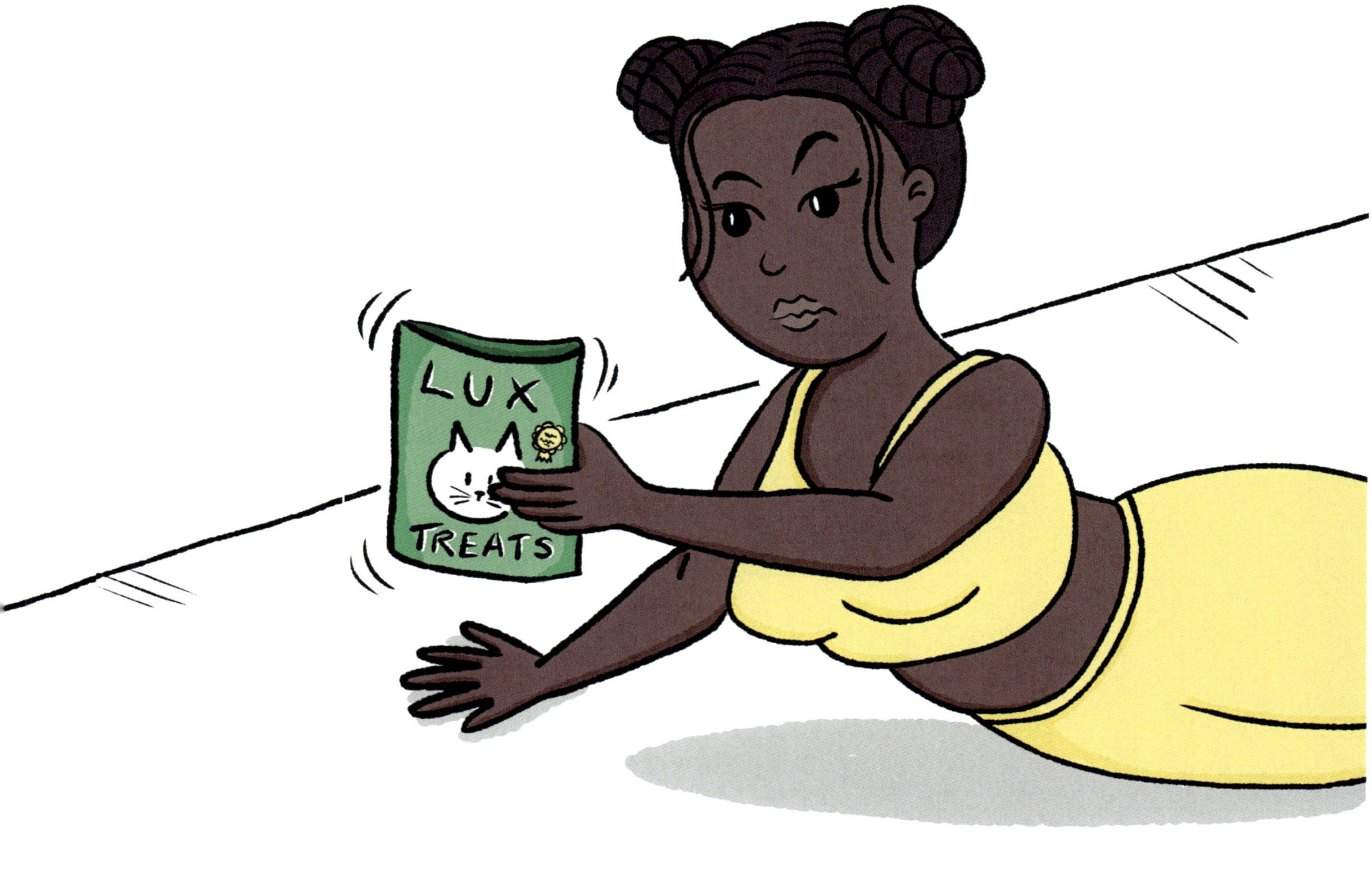
LUX
TREATS

The mornings were funny when Mick went to work. Banger sat by the door with his Cheshire cat **smirk**.

"*See you **later**, Chump*." He'd tip Mick his hat. "*Just bring home the **bacon***," meowed Banger the cat.

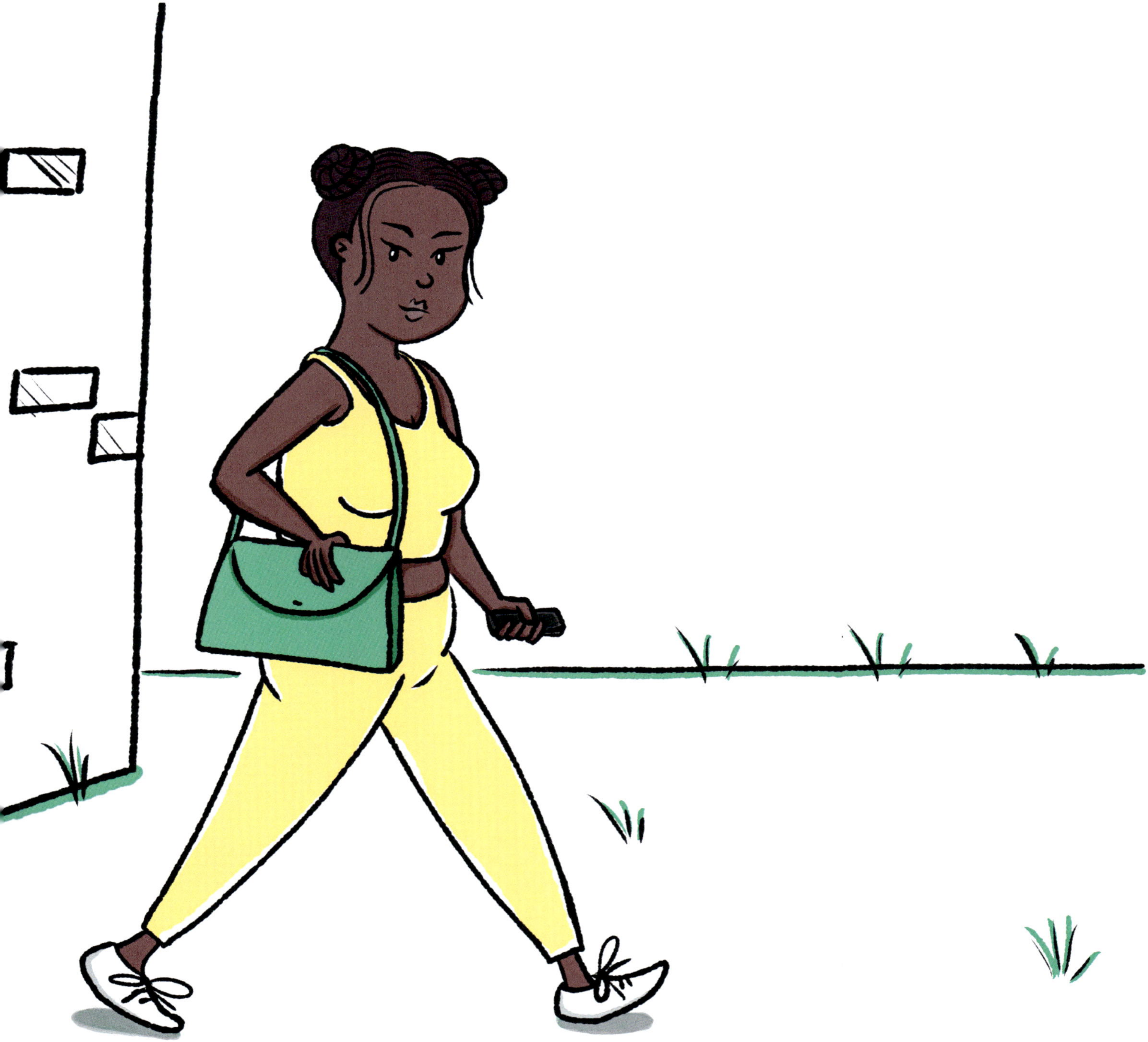

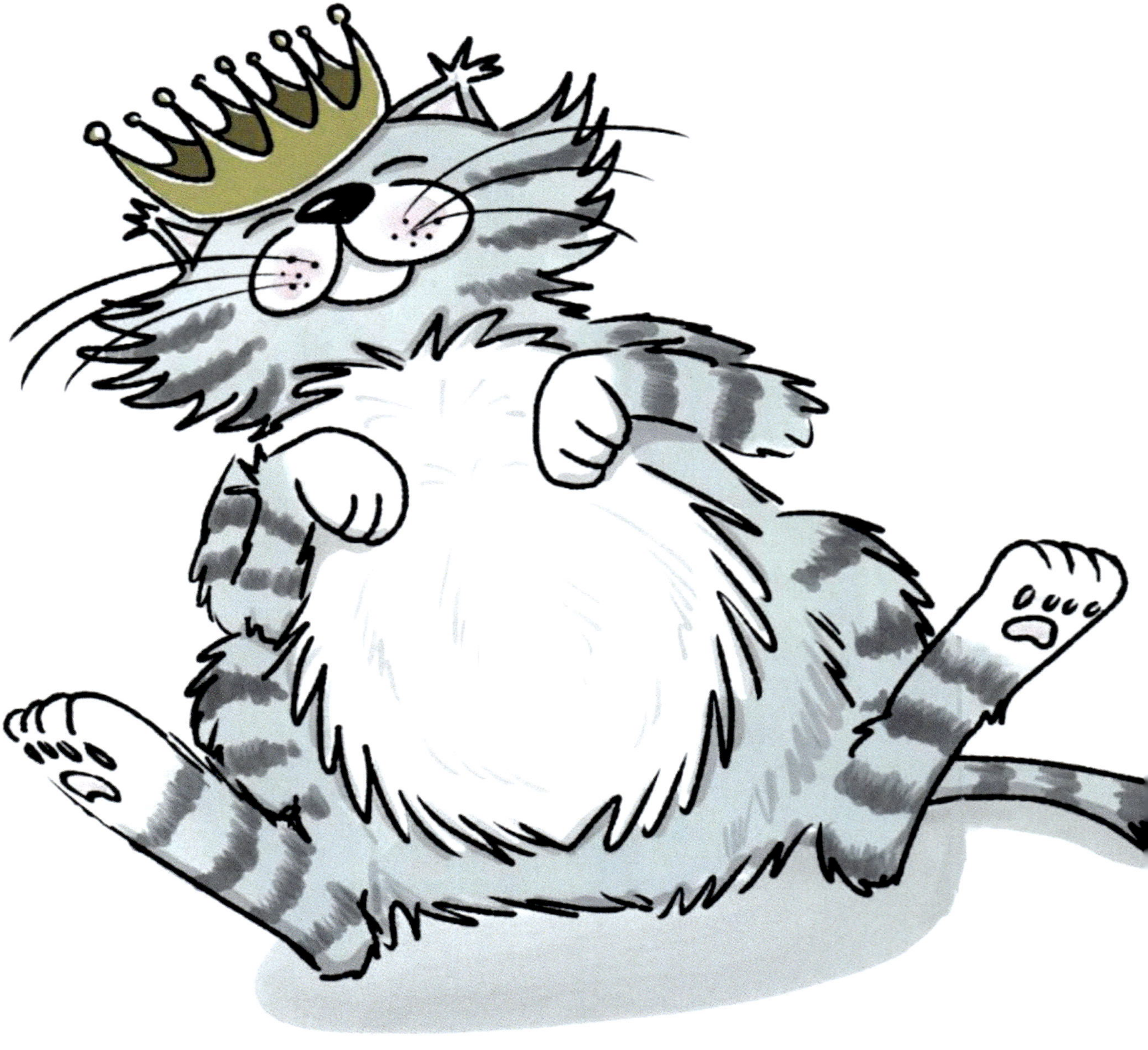

Since Banger arrived life was turned **upside-down**

He took over our home. Yes! He wore the crown.

This once scrawny feline became plump

…no, **FAT**!

Living the high life was **Banger** the cat.

And just like that, Banger was the undisputed ruler of our apartment. It is also how we became pet owners!

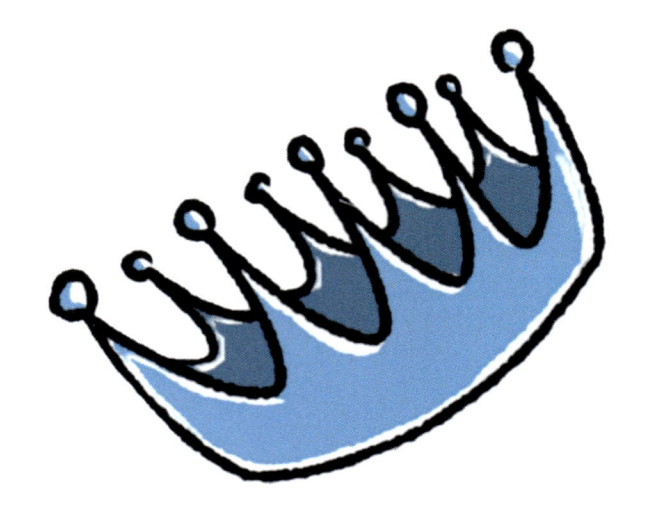

Did you adopt your pet?

Or did your pet adopt you?

Tell us your story.

Write to us at: anniemack@omerapress.com

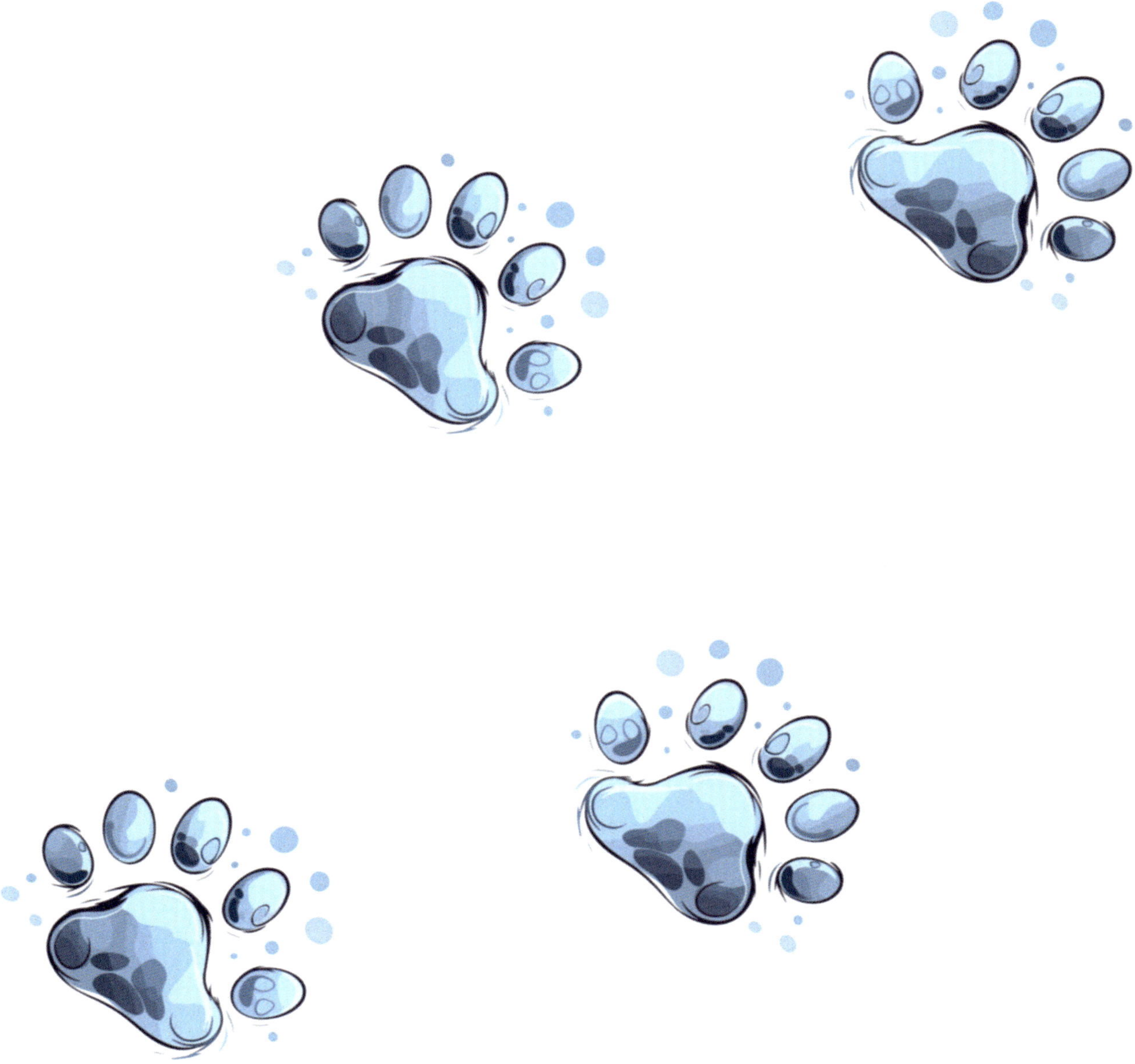

Why was the cat sitting on the computer?

Because it wanted to keep an eye on the mouse!

What did the cat say when it lost all its money?

"I'm paw!"

What do you call a cat who loves the beach?

Sandy Claws!

What do you call a cat who loves to bowl?

An alley cat!

Annie's Paws-itive Thoughts

Adopting a pet is a super experience! It's like inviting a new member into your family. Cats and dogs are experts at giving cuddles and kisses, especially when you're feeling down. They're always there to snuggle up with you and make you feel better.

Pets make awesome friends, too. They'll play games with you, go on exciting adventures, and even watch your favourite shows. And did you know that spending time with pets is great for your mental health? Just petting them makes you feel warm and fuzzy inside. Plus, when you take care of a pet, like feeding them and giving them love, it teaches you to be responsible and caring, building your character along the way. Pets are incredibly loyal, sticking by your side through thick and thin, always ready to offer comfort with a purr or a wag of their tail.

When you adopt a pet from a shelter, you're doing something truly special. You're giving a furry friend a second chance at happiness! Many pets in shelters are looking for loving homes, and by adopting them, you're giving them a forever family. It's like becoming a superhero for animals! So, if you're thinking about getting a pet, remember that adopting is a paws-itively amazing way to make a difference in an animal's life.

Are you thinking of getting a pet?

If you're thinknig of getting a pet, it's essential to consider factors such as the type of pet you want, your lifestyle, and your ability to provide proper care and attention before making a decision. Additionally, always prioritize adopting from reputable sources that emphasize the welfare of the animals.

Common Places to Get Pets

Here are some common places where people can get pets:

Rescue Organizations: Rescue organizations specialize in finding homes for specific types of animals or breeds. They rescue animals from various situations, such as neglect or abandonment, and work to find them loving homes.

Animal Shelters: Shelters are dedicated to finding homes for animals in need. They often have a variety of pets available for adoption, including cats, dogs, rabbits, and more.

Breeders: Responsible breeders selectively breed animals to produce healthy and well-socialized pets. It's essential to do thorough research to find a reputable breeder who prioritizes the health and well-being of their animals.

Pet Stores: Some pet stores sell animals such as fish, birds, small mammals, and reptiles. However, it's important to ensure that these stores source their animals ethically and provide proper care for them.

Friends and Family: Sometimes, friends or family members may have pets that they need to rehome due to various circumstances. Adopting from someone you know can be a great way to give a pet a loving home.

Foster Programs: Some shelters and rescue organizations have foster programs where animals are placed in temporary homes until they find their forever families. Adopting from a foster program allows you to provide a home for a pet in need while also giving you the opportunity to learn more about their personality and needs.

Annie Mack (Author)

Annie had an innate gift for spinning tales from the moment she could talk, and she imagined her stories would one day find a place in the world of literature.

Fascinated with the intricacies of life, Annie earned a BSc in Molecular Biology and Genetics from Guelph University. At the same time, she cultivated her love of books, specializing in English and Children's Literature. With a finesse for blending the scientific and the literary, Annie's distinct writing style and voice resonate throughout her stories.

Diverse executive roles took Annie continent hopping: travelling European landscapes, embracing the vibrant cultures of Trinidad & Tobago, and crisscrossing the United States and Canada. Each place was a source of inspiration and understanding of the histories and cultures that shape some of her characters.

> *"Being at the beck and call of my fur pal, Banger, was highly entertaining. Pets become family members and have a unique way of brightening our day. I hope you enjoyed reading about how Banger touched our lives. Love up your pets!"* – Annie M.

Phillip Reed (illustrator)

Phillip was determined to become an accomplished illustrator. But influenced by societal norms, he heeded his mother's advice to pursue 'a proper job.'

For three decades, Phillip spent his time navigating a myriad of administrative and management roles. However, he remained steadfast in his artistic quest and acquired qualifications in both art and creative writing.

Phillip's newfound expertise secured publication opportunities in magazines, which he then expanded into the world of children's literature. His artistic journey is a testament to the power of his unwavering passion and the resilience of his creative spirit.

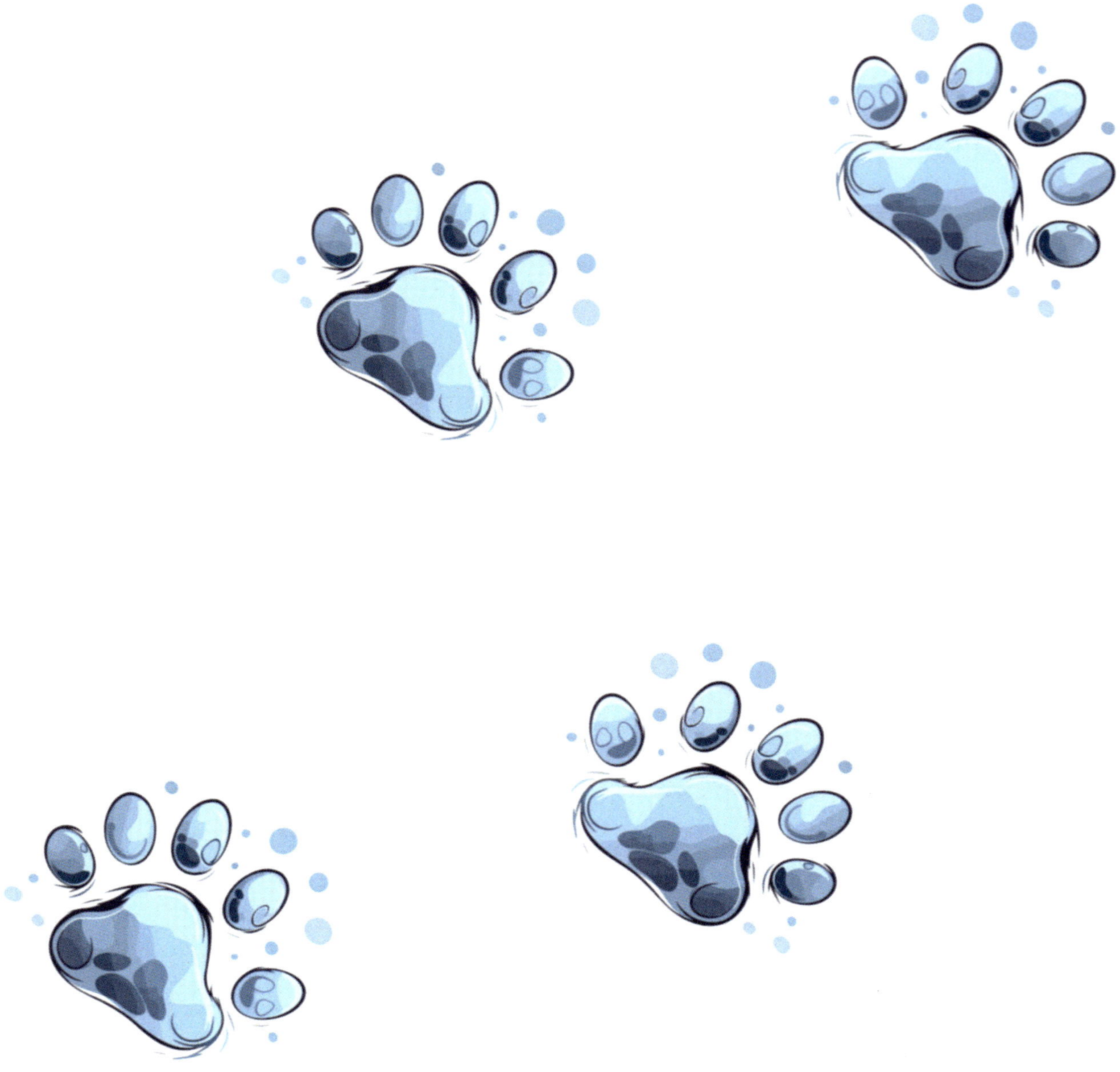

WHAT'S NEXT

Hey there, bookworms! Dive into the pages of our website and here's what you'll find:

Explore Our World

A treasure trove of stories, puzzles, and cool "How To" guides made just for you! From thrilling tales to mind-bending challenges, there's something for everyone.

Monthly Giveaways

Don't miss out on our draws where you can win awesome prizes like books and super cool T-shirts! Keep your eyes peeled for details on how to enter.

www.omerapress.com

omera

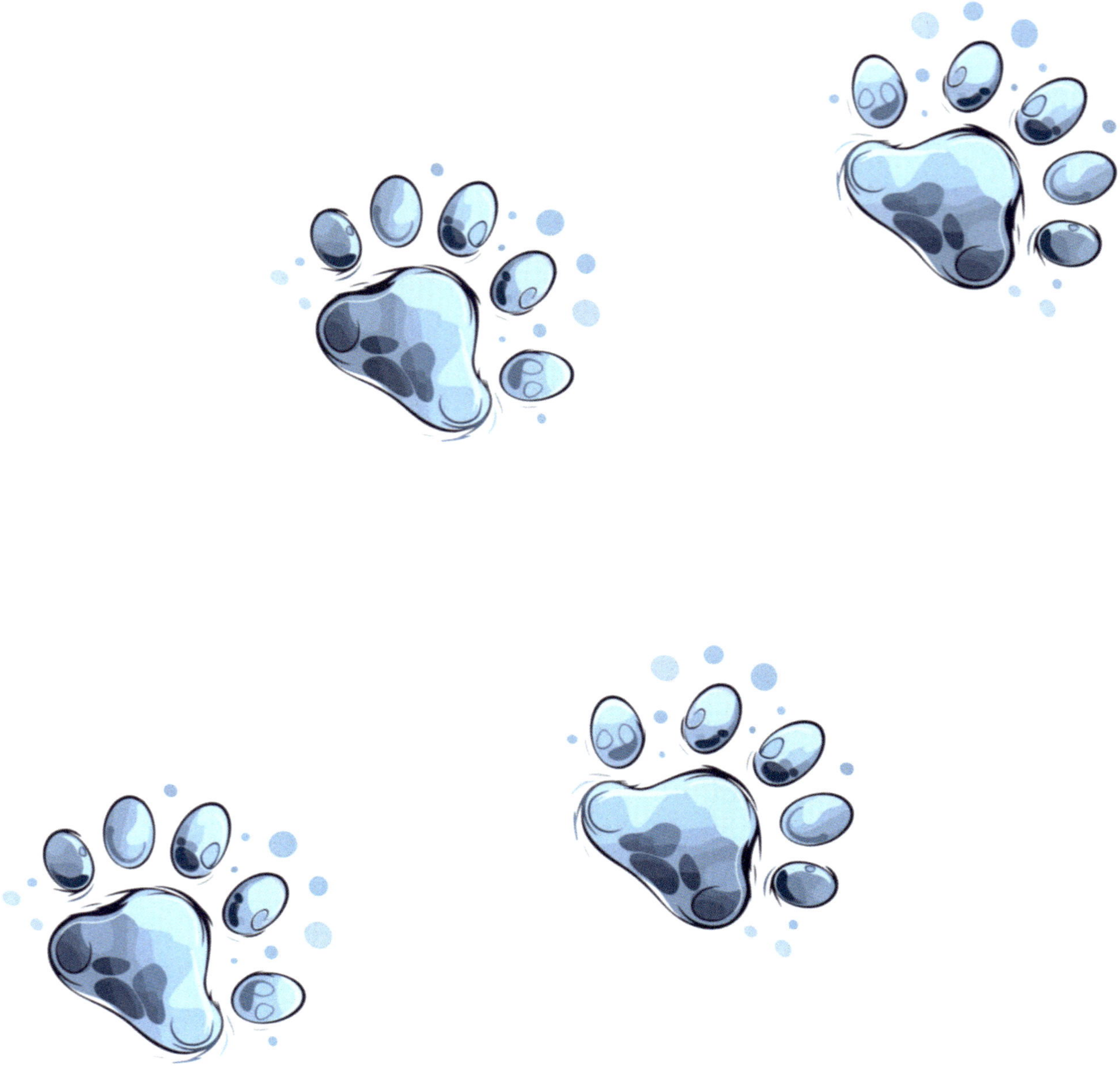

CHECK OUT OTHER ANNIE MACK STORIES

The Chronicles of Burning Candles Series:
#1 A Case of Stolen Dreams (2023)

The Ickyology Series:
#1 Oh No It's SNOT: When A Nostril Goes Viral (2024)

A High-Flying Hiccup (2024)

omera

THE END

Manufactured by Amazon.ca
Bolton, ON